LET'S RIDE!

DRAGSTERS

MARIE ROGERS

PowerKiDS press.

NEW YORK

Published in 2022 by The Rosen Publishing Group, Inc.
29 East 21st Street, New York, NY 10010

First Edition

Portions of this work were originally authored by J. Poolos and published as *Wild About Dragsters*. All new material in this edition was authored by Marie Rogers.

Editor: Kate Mikoley
Book Design: Rachel Rising

Photo Credits: Cover Michael Stokes/Shutterstock.com; Cover, p.1 absemetov/Shutterstock.com; Cover, pp. 1, 3, 4, 6, 8, 10, 12, 14, 16, 18, 20, 22, 23, 24 StarLine/Shutterstock.com; p. 4 dan_prat/E+/Getty Images; pp. 5, 6, 8, 17 Icon Sportswire/Contributor/Getty Images; pp. 7, 9, 11, 15, 21 Icon Sports Wire/Contributor/Icon Sportswire/Getty Images; p. 10 Volodymyr Horbovyy/iStock/Getty Images Plus/Getty Images; pp. 13, 19 The Enthusiast Network/Contributor/Getty Images; p. 14 Creatas/Getty Images; p.16 ChrisBoswell/iStock/Getty Images Plus/Getty Images; p. 20 FrankRamspott/E+/Getty Images.

Some of the images in this book illustrate individuals who are models. The depictions do not imply actual situations or events.

Library of Congress Cataloging-in-Publication Data

Names: Rogers, Marie, 1990- author.
Title: Dragsters / Marie Rogers.
Description: New York : PowerKids Press, [2022] | Series: Let's ride! | Includes index.
Identifiers: LCCN 2020045773 | ISBN 9781725327351 (library binding) | ISBN 9781725327337 (paperback) | ISBN 9781725327344 (6 pack)
Subjects: LCSH: Dragsters–Juvenile literature.
Classification: LCC TL236.2 .R64 2022 | DDC 629.228/5–dc23
LC record available at https://lccn.loc.gov/2020045773

Manufactured in the United States of America

CPSIA Compliance Information: Batch #CSPK22. For Further Information contact Rosen Publishing, New York, New York at 1-800-237-9932.

CONTENTS

READY, SET, GO!

Imagine going from 0 to 100 miles (0 to 161 km) per hour in less than one second. It might sound impossible, but that's how fast the speediest dragsters go! Dragsters are **vehicles** used in drag races. In a drag race, two dragsters race down a straight track to the finish line.

Dragsters are built to go fast. They leave the race's starting line in a cloud of tire smoke. Just five to ten seconds later the race is over.

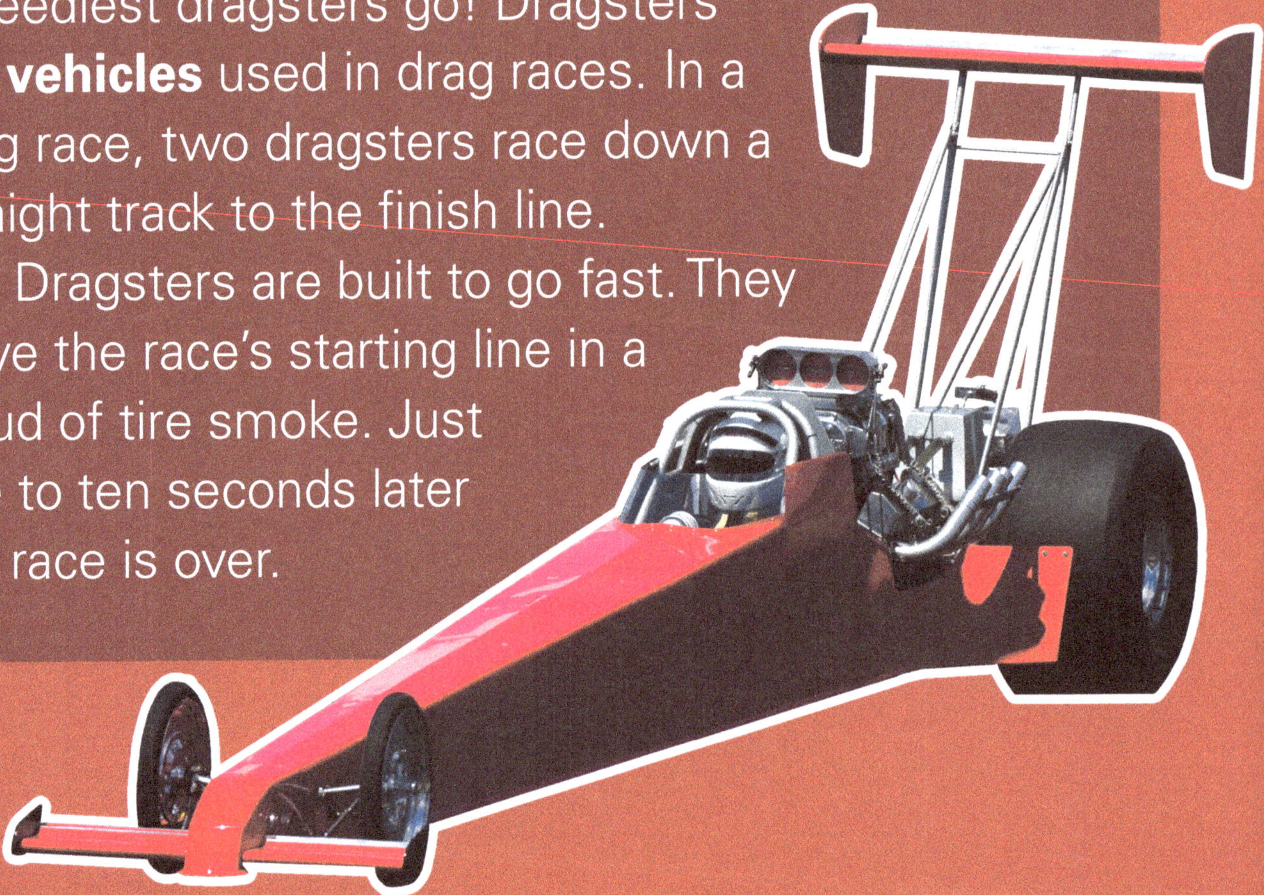

There are several different kinds of dragsters. Top **Fuel** dragsters are the fastest!

TOP OF THE GAME

Top Fuel dragsters can go faster than 330 miles (531 km) per hour! These dragsters are long, thin cars with small, narrow front wheels. They're low to the ground and have powerful engines that make more than 10,000 **horsepower**.

All Top Fuel dragsters must weigh at least 2,330 pounds (1,057 kg). A giant wing at the back helps keep them on the track. These dragsters are so fast that they need two **parachutes** to help slow them down after crossing the finish line!

Top Fuel cars are 25 feet (7.6 m) long. The back tires are much bigger than the front ones.

WHAT'S SO FUNNY?

Another popular kind of dragster is called a Funny Car. One way to tell Funny Cars and Top Fuel dragsters apart is that only Funny Cars have roofs and **windshields**. Funny Cars' back wheels are big and wide. Their front wheels are small and narrow.

In general, Funny Cars are usually a bit slower than Top Fuel dragsters. However, these cars can sometimes go faster than 330 miles (531 km) too! Their powerful engines make around 8,000 horsepower.

Like Top Fuel dragsters, Funny Cars use parachutes to slow them down and help them come to a stop.

FUEL UP!

Dragsters have very powerful engines. **Mechanics** sometimes change the cars' original engines to make them more powerful. One way to make a dragster go faster is to add a supercharger or turbocharger. These parts force more air into the engine. This lets the engine burn more fuel to go faster.

Most dragster engines burn high-powered gas. Some use **alcohol**. Top Fuel dragsters burn nitromethane. This is a powerful and **explosive** fuel that makes the cars go especially fast.

Top Fuel dragsters let off clouds of smoke and light. This is because of the nitromethane.

DRAG RACING HISTORY

Drag racing got its start in Southern California in the 1930s. Early drivers raced in dry lake beds. In 1938, a man named Wally Parks helped form the Southern California Timing Association to **organize** and oversee races.

The first official drag strip, or track, opened in 1950 in Santa Ana, California. In 1951, Parks founded the National Hot Rod Association (NHRA) to make classes and safety rules for different kinds of cars. Today, the NHRA is the leading organization in professional drag racing.

The NHRA held its first national event in 1955. This dragster was at the group's third yearly event in 1957.

OFF TO THE RACES

Dragsters are grouped into classes based on car type and speed. This way, dragsters race against other cars that are about the same size and have the same kind of engine.

For years, a standard NHRA track was 1,320 feet (400 m), or a quarter mile, long. In 2008, the NHRA cut the **distance** to 1,000 feet (305 m). Two dragsters race at a time. The winner races against another dragster. The driver who makes it through all the races is the overall winner.

Driving a dragster is dangerous, or unsafe. Drivers must always wear a helmet and seatbelt.

START YOUR ENGINES!

A drag race starts with a Christmas tree—but don't expect there to be gifts. In drag racing, a Christmas tree is a tool with lights that tell the racers when to go. It sits on the starting line between the two cars.

When the green light flashes, the cars are off! Drivers change **gears** many times throughout the short race. The fastest dragsters cross the finish line in just 5 seconds! Then, it's time to let out the parachutes.

Sometimes, fuel leaving the dragster causes flames to leap out of the **exhaust pipes**.

GETTING SAFER WITH GARLITS

"Big Daddy" Don Garlits started racing in the 1950s. He's still one of the most famous names in drag racing today.

Garlits was a fast racer who made the sport safer too. Dragster engines were at the car's front until 1970. That year, Garlits lost half of his right foot when his dragster's engine blew up. While healing, he came up with an idea to put the engine in the back. Because of Garlits's idea, dragsters are now safer than before!

Garlits was also the first dragster driver to wear a full-body suit that kept him safer from fire. Today, these are regularly worn.

RACE ON!

It's not only Top Fuel dragsters and Funny Cars that drag race. Pro Stock dragsters look like everyday cars but have much more powerful engines. They're much faster than cars you see on the road. Pro Stock motorcycles have strong engines and can reach nearly 200 miles (322 km) per hour.

Drag racing isn't just for drivers—it's for fans too! Many people enjoy going to drag races. If you go to a race, bring **earplugs**. Dragsters are some of the loudest cars around!

Pro Stock motorcycles have bars that reach behind their back wheel, called wheelie bars. These keep the motorcycles from flipping over.

GLOSSARY

alcohol: A clear fuel that pours and burns easily.

distance: The measured space between two places or things.

earplug: A piece of soft matter that can be put in the ear to keep out noise.

exhaust pipe: A tube through which the smoky air made by burning gas or other fuels escapes from the engine.

explosive: A kind of matter or device that produces a powerful blast.

fuel: Something used to make energy, heat, or power.

gear: A part of a machine that helps it work.

horsepower: The measure of the power produced by an engine.

mechanic: A person who builds and fixes machines.

organize: To put together in an orderly way.

parachute: A specially shaped piece of cloth that collects air to slow something down.

vehicle: An object that moves people from one place to another.

windshield: A sheet of glass that goes across the front of a car, truck, plane, or boat.

For More Information

Books

Fishman, Jon M. *Cool Drag Racing Cars*. Minneapolis, MN: Lerner Publications, 2019.

Roselius, J. Chris. *Superfast Drag Racing*. Minneapolis, MN: Lerner Publications, 2020.

Websites

Don Garlits Museum of Drag Racing
garlits.com
Check out this website to learn more about Don Garlits, look at photos of cars at the museum, and read about people in the Hall of Fame.

NHRA 101
www.nhra.com/nhra-101
Read about the basics of drag racing on the NHRA's website.

Publisher's note to educators and parents: Our editors have carefully reviewed these websites to ensure that they are suitable for students. Many websites change frequently, however, and we cannot guarantee that a site's future contents will continue to meet our high standards of quality and educational value. Be advised that students should be closely supervised whenever they access the internet.

INDEX